GUARANTEED-
SLEEPO

Hi! Ready for a fantastic sleepover? Good, because this is one sleepover party that can't miss. Why? Because everything you need for a dusk-till-dawn blast is right here. This book is your guided tour through hours of nonstop fun. You'll find flashy fashion tips, yummy tummy pleasers, things that will make you laugh . . . and scary stuff to send delicious goose bumps up your arms. There are games, jokes, and ideas, silly scripts, video rental suggestions . . . well, just flip through and see for yourself!

Sleepover hostesses will want to look at the party planner in the back—but that's the only thing you need to do ahead. The rest of the fun happens while the party is going on. Just open to any page and pick an activity, or go through the book chapter by chapter. No matter what, you'll have a wonderful time till the wee hours of the morning.

So let's get started! Ready, set, go . . . it's sleepover time!

Super Sleepover Kit

By Daniella Burr

PARACHUTE
PRESS, INC.

PARACHUTE PRESS, INC.
200 FIFTH AVENUE
NEW YORK, NY 10010

First printing: August 1988
Printed in the USA

Design by Michel Design
Cover Photo: James Kent Kittle

TABLE OF CONTENTS

PARTY STARTERS

The big night has finally arrived. You've got the friends, the flicks, and the food. But the excitement is missing. You are all just sitting around, waiting for something to happen. Never fear, the answer to your problem is here! These icebreakers are a surefire way to keep your sleepover party from being a real snooze!

Let's get this party going!

Rigamarole

You'll need a pencil and paper for this one. Why? Well ... it's a long story.

One guest writes the first two lines of a story on the paper. When she is through, the first author should fold down the paper so that only the second line of the story shows. The first author hands the paper to the next girl. She adds two more lines to the story and covers all the lines but the last one. Then she passes it to the next person. Keep going until the page is full. Then read the "story" out loud. It may not make much sense, but it's sure to get you giggling—especially if you all name the characters after your sleepover pals!

Starstruck!

You'll see stars when you play this fun question and answer icebreaking game.

Send one person out of the room. That person will be "It." The rest of the gang then picks a famous movie, music, or TV star. Once everyone has decided on a star, call the person who is It back into the room.

The person who is It has to guess the identity of the secret celebrity. She does that by asking questions about the star like "What color does this person remind you of?" Or "If this person were an animal, what would he or she be?"

Keep playing until everyone has had a chance to be It.

Twisted Pretzel

This game is sure to start a tight circle of friendship!

Everyone stands in a circle. Each girl uses her right hand to hold the hand of a person that is not standing next to her. Then each girl grabs the left hand of a different person in the circle.

Got it? Now everyone has to work together to make a perfect circle, with each girl winding up next to the girl whose hands she's holding now. Sound easy? Here comes the tough part—no one can let go of the hands they are holding right now! You have to make the circle by climbing over and under each other's arms, twisting around, crawling under each other's legs, whatever it takes!

To Tell the Truth Test

If you've had enough tests in school this week, you may be tempted to pass this one by. But don't—it's strictly for laughs. Take it and see.

Each girl grabs a piece of paper and a pencil. Someone reads each of the questions out loud. After you've all written down your answers, check the results at the end of the test— that's when the jokes really begin!

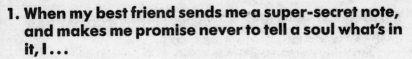

1. When my best friend sends me a super-secret note, and makes me promise never to tell a soul what's in it, I...

A. Read the note over the school public address system.

B. Rent a billboard and plaster the note over Route 51.

C. Chew the note fifty times and swallow it.

2. On rainy days I like to...

A. Count raindrops.

B. Send nasty letters to TV weathermen.

C. Gab on the phone for hours.

3. If I had a million dollars, I would...

A. Start a millionaire kids club. I would be president, of course.

B. Hire U2 to play at a huge party in my honor.

C. Start a fund to feed the hungry and give shelter to the homeless.

4. My very best friend comes to school with her hair looking an absolute mess, so I . . .

   A. Find her a pretty bag to put over her head.

   B. Introduce her as my new alien friend from Venus.

   C. Grab her and pull her into the ladies' room, where the two of us try a quick new hairstyle.

5. If I could be any animal, I would be a . . .

   A. Drone bee working in a hive.

   B. Fluffy French poodle named Fifi, who eats designer dog food from a silver tray.

   C. Unicorn.

6. At this moment I wish I could . . .

   A. Stop taking this stupid test.

   B. Flap my arms and fly to Mars.

   C. Find the answer to world peace.

7. When I am depressed, I . . .

   A. Clip my toenails.

   B. Eat an ice cream sundae the size of Mount Rushmore.

   C. Read the newspaper and think of people with worse problems than I have.

8. My favorite spare-time activity is...

A. Dancing with a broom.

B. Digging tunnels to China in my backyard.

C. Cleaning out my closet.

9. I really like the new kid in town. To get him to notice me and ask for a date, I...

A. Sleep in a tent on his front porch.

B. Tell him I am really a foreign princess, and it is his patriotic duty to ask me out for the sake of the foreign relations between my country and the United States.

C. Ask him if he'd like a tour of his new city and offer to introduce him to some of my friends.

10. If the TV is broken, I like to...

A. Watch the radio instead.

B. Work on my latest romance novel—a thrilling story of a girl and her scooter.

C. Help my little brother with his math homework.

To find out what this test reveals about you, just turn the page.

Test Results

Here's the truth about you!
    Give yourself 1 point for every question you answered with an A, 5 points for every question you answered with a B, and 10 points for every question you answered with a C.

1-33 points: Your score indicates that you are the kind of person that gets a kick out of watching the grass grow or watching the men unload the Brussels sprouts at the local fruit stand. Perhaps you should try a career in the circus as the human hamster running in the wheel.

34-65 points: What a wild imagination you have! You have an exciting life ahead of you. Your name will be in lights, and your picture will be plastered in post offices the world over!

66-100 points: A score this high proves you are a sensible kid with a good head on her shoulders—but are you sure the head is yours? No kid could be this perfect!

AMAZING MAKEOVERS

Makeovers are a must for every sleepover! And when it comes to marvelous makeovers, it pays to start at the top—with your hair! After all, tonight is a special night—it deserves a special hairstyle!

Sudsy Soapy Sculptures!

Some artists sculpt with clay, others with stone. You can be a sculptor, too—Sudsy Soapy Sculptures can make your hair a work of art.

Start by lathering up your hair with your favorite shampoo. (Make sure you drape a towel around your shoulders to keep your nightshirt from getting wet.) Once your hair is completely covered in sudsy shampoo lather, try molding your hair into different shapes. Make it stand straight up, or curl or swirl. It will stay just where you put it. If you think your new style is a total washout, don't worry, it will wash out!

7

Super Spikes

Calling all short-haired sleepover pals! You will be sure to get the punky point if you try this sassy, spiky style.

Rub styling gel all through your hair. Then quickly, before the gel has a chance to dry, slide your fingers through your hair, picking up clumps of hair and holding them straight out. When the spikes are in place, spray hairspray all through your hair.

(Always shut your eyes when spraying hairspray in the front of your hair.) The hairspray will keep your hair in place while it dries.

Hint: For the perfect punk look, try a few streaks of washable color—maybe a nice orange or green. Be sure to check the label to make sure the spray color will wash out with shampoo. This isn't the look you want for school on Monday!

Bravo for Braids!

When it comes to long hair, you don't have to twist your brain to come up with a terrific do. Just twist your long locks into this terrific twisted braid!

Gather all your hair at the top of your head and pull it over to the right side. Begin braiding, gently twisting the front section so you have a soft smooth roll from your left ear to your braid. Some hair mousse or gel will help keep the roll in place.

We're Just Ribbon You!

For beautiful hair with a colorful twist, why not add a ribbon to your braid?

Start by dividing your hair into three sections, just as you would for any other braid. Wrap a ribbon around and around the middle section of the braid, like the stripe on a candy cane. Then braid your hair as usual.

Phenomenal Phrizz!

For a wild funky look—the long and short of it is frizz! It's easy to make any length of hair a frizz phenomenon.

Start with your hair wet. Divide your hair into tiny sections. Then braid each tiny section into small braids. End each braid with a coated rubber band. Wait until your hair is completely dry. Spray each braid with hairspray. Wait for the spray to dry. Remove the coated rubber bands from the braids and comb out your hair.

Hint: For an extra frizz flair, wait until the braids dry, and spray just a few of them with colors that wash out with shampoo.

Ooo-La-La!

When it comes to fashion, no one does it better than the French. To give yourself a bit of that famous French flair, ask someone at the party to help you French braid your hair. Sometimes this is hard to do yourself. Your friendly French hairdresser (or sleepover pal) can follow these simple instructions. The result is sure to be magnifique!

1. Brush the front and side hair to the top of your head and hold it as if you were about to gather it into a high ponytail. Leave the rest of the hair loose. Eventually you are going to braid the loose part into the braid.

2. Separate the top part into three sections and start to braid.

3. Bit by bit, add sections of the loose hair into the three sections you are braiding. The trick is to keep picking up the lower hair and pulling it into your original three sections as the braid moves down. Do this in equal parts, and be sure to do it before the top strands of hair are too short or thin.

4. When you've reached the end of your braid, secure it with a clip or covered rubber band. You can tuck the ends under with bobby pins or attach a pretty bow at the end.

Hint: This style works best with long, one-length hair. If hair has short layers on top, let them curl freely (or set them) and start your braid where the layers are longer.

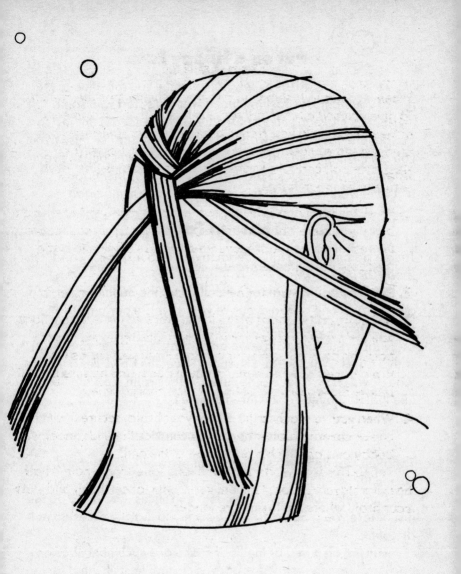

Put on a Happy Face

Now that you've got heavenly hair, it's time you faced up to the rest of your fantastic fashion makeover. Let's start with some mysterious makeup secrets! Of course, these secrets are just for sleepovers. You'd never want to be seen in public like this. When you get through with this silly sleepover makeover, pull out your instant camera and take pictures—then destroy them. You wouldn't want anyone to use them as blackmail material!

Face-up Facial

There's nothing like a little steam to make your skin rosy and ready for makeup.

Start by boiling water. Carefully pour the boiling water into a bowl. Add one or two drops of your favorite perfume (don't overdo it) or a drop or two of lemon juice.

Wash your face with soap and water, then cover your head with a towel. With the towel hanging over the bowl like a tent, lean down so your face is about six inches from the water. Stay like that for no more than three minutes.

Cute as a Cucumber

To soften that delicate skin near your eyes, all you need is a cucumber.

Carefully cut the cucumber into thin slices. Be sure to do this just before you plan on using the slices, so that the slices do not dry out.

Lay flat on a bed or the floor. Place one cucumber slice on each eye. Be sure to keep your eyes closed! Rest like that for five minutes.

The Eyes Have It!

"Look into my eyes." That's the famous movie line. Everyone will be looking at your eyes when you try these totally outrageous eye tips.

A lightning bolt will give your eyes an electrifying effect! Use black eyeliner to draw a lightning bolt about an inch and a half from your eye. Then follow the outside line of the lightning bolt with blue or green eye shadow. Eye shadow with glitter in it will make your eyes really light up a room!

Cat's eyes will really bring out the animal in you. Use eyeliner to carefully draw an outline along your eyelid (just above the lashes) and along the bottom of your eye (just under your lower lashes). Let the two lines meet at a point by your temple. Color in the area between your eyes and your temple with stripes of exotic eye shadows. The effect will be MEOW-WOW!

You're Blushing!

It's easy to give your cheeks a dramatic flush. All you need is some basic blush and a little bit of gold glitter.

Start by putting the blush on your cheeks. Always start from just below your cheekbone and brush the blush up on a diagonal to your ear. Then add a touch of blush to your temple area.

Put a little water on your cheekbones. Then gently dab a drop of glitter on your cheekbones. The water will make it stick. A little glitter is enough—gobs of glitter look just awful!

Hit the Nail on the Head

Enough of this silliness. The makeup experiments you've just done are only for sleepovers. You can wash them off before anyone catches you. But nice nails are something you can take home with you tomorrow morning. A good manicure usually costs a fortune, but here are a few tips for an easy handy-dandy manicure you guys can try tonight for free. It really works!

Remove any nail polish from your nails. Be sure to get it all off—even the tricky stuff by the sides! File your nails with an emery board. Always file upward from the corners of your nails to the tips. Shape your nails into perfectly rounded ovals. Then soak your hands for a few minutes in warm sudsy water.

Next, break the cotton off of a cotton swab. Use the stick part to gently clean the underside of your nail. Then use the stick to gently push back your cuticles. Add a drop of talcum powder to your nails. Use a soft cloth to gently rub each nail until it shines!

For a fancy touch, apply some colored nail polish. Top it off with clear polish. Have polish remover handy to clean up any smudges. (Put the remover on cotton swabs.)

FASHION FLAIR

Even the most heavenly hair and the most fabulous face won't make you a fashion 10 unless you have the right clothes. Here's an easy idea for creating fun and funky sleepover fashions. There's no better time than right now for living out your fashion fantasies!

If you've followed the instructions on your sleepover invitation, you should all have brought that one outfit you really can't stand—you know the one: it's usually stuck in the back of your closet—and one accessory, like a hat or a belt, to the party.

Bet you were wondering why you had to cart all that stuff over to the party. Well, you are about to find out. Put all the clothes and accessories into one big pile. Let everyone take turns mixing and matching tops, bottoms, and accessories. Experiment. The wilder the better! One girl's trash can be another girl's treasure.

The Fashion Parade

Now that you look spectacular, it's time for the all-exciting Sleepover Spectacular—the Fashion Parade.

Everyone lines up backstage (another room will do). The narrator stands to the side of the stage as the models come down the runway one at a time. The narrator announces each model and describes her outfit.

Here's an example of what we mean.

Narrator: Our first model is Jennifer. Jennifer's hobbies include horseback riding and collecting chocolate bars. This outfit is designed by her favorite French designer, Coco Crispies Chanel! Rumor has it that Jennifer has a separate house in Palm Springs—just to hold all her millions of outfits and shoes. Jennifer, is there any truth to the tale that you are the nation's foremost clotheshorse?

Jennifer: Neigh!

Narrator: You heard it here first, folks! Now it's time for Jennifer to trot on over to Paris, where she is sure to buy up half the fashions in this year's spring show.

And now, here comes Amy, our next model. Amy's outfit is something new this year from famed designer Cow-man Klein. You've heard of animal-print clothing? Well, this is animal-scent clothing. It's for the woman who knows where she's going, but still wants everyone to remember where she's been! This scentsational animal-scent outfit would fit in anywhere—from a jungle safari to a trip to the zoo. (Holding her nose) Pee-yoo-tiful, Amy!

Our next beauty is Dee-Dee. Dee-Dee's look is futuristic, part of the Fashions From Space line created by the designer for the NASA Space Program, Liz Airborne! The look is perfect for Dee-Dee, since she's often found mooning over the cutest guy in school!

Our final model is Lisa. Her outfit is designed by Guess?

Voice from the audience: Who?

Narrator: Guess!

Voice: I don't know. Who?

Narrator: Guess! Oh, never mind! Lisa is new to this country. Lovely Lisa only speaks one word of English. But she tries to use it whenever she can. It's the foremost word in fashion today. Lisa . . .

Lisa: (Waving) Buy! Buy!

Narrator: Bye-bye to you, too, Lisa. And bye-bye to you! Thanks for coming to our Sleepover Spectacular 1989!

MORE GOOD-TIME GAMES

Facts Only a Friend Could Know!

You think you know your friends pretty well, huh? Well, that knowledge could be worth big points when you play this fun game.

Now is the time for all best friends to form teams of two. The hostess of this party can't play; she must be the mistress of ceremonies. One half of each pair should go into the next room (this will serve as our soundproof booth). The other partner must write down the answers to the questions below on a pad of paper. The mistress of ceremonies will read each question out loud, then call the other girls back into the room and ask them to guess what their best friend answered. A correct answer earns the pair five points.

After all the questions have been answered, it's time for the big switch. Send the other girls out of the room, and try the same thing again. The pair with the most points at the end of the game wins.

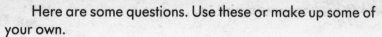

Here are some questions. Use these or make up some of your own.

1. Ever since I can remember, my friend has had a crush on...

_____

2. My friend's favorite teacher is...

_____

3. If my friend could be anyone in the world, she would be...

_____

_____

4. My friend's favorite TV show is...

_____

5. If my friend could have one toy back from when she was a baby, it would be her...

_____

_____

6. If my friend could change one thing about herself, it would be her...

_____

_____

7. My friend's favorite album is...

_____

8. My friend refuses to wear anything that is...

_____

_____

9. My friend's worst habit is . . .

_____

_____

10. My friend's family has a secret nickname for her. I know it, too. They call her . . .

_____

11. When my friend is hungry she likes to eat . . .

_____

12. My friend's favorite song is . . .

_____

13. On her dream date my friend would go out with . . .

_____

14. My friend's life could best be described by which of these movie titles? _Down and Out in Beverly Hills_, _The Good, the Bad, and the Ugly_, or _The Little Princess._

_____

15. When she is really nervous, my friend usually does this . . .

_____

Dare Ya!

Sometimes it is tough to tell the truth. But sometimes it is easier to tell the truth than to pay the consequences for keeping your mouth shut. That's especially true when you play this truth-seeking game.

Everyone sits in a circle. Now each girl gets a chance to ask another girl a really personal question. The girl who is being asked has the choice of answering the question or taking a dare. If she answers the question, her turn is over and it is the next girl's chance to ask a question. But if she refuses to answer the question, she must take the dare!

Make sure every girl has a chance to ask and answer at least one question.

Here are some daring dares for you and your friends to try.

1. **Hop on one foot and sing the theme from *The Brady Bunch*.**

2. **Imitate Bruce Springsteen singing *Born in the USA*.**

3. **Do your best imitation of a dog who wants to be fed.**

4. **Stand on a chair and belt out *The Flintstones* theme song in your best Fred Flintstone voice.**

5. **Count backwards from 100 by threes while rubbing your tummy.**

6. **Skip around the room singing *I'm a Yankee Doodle Dandy*.**

7. **Sing a hit song as if you were Alvin of Alvin and the Chipmunks.**

8. **Pretend you are a squirrel cracking a nut that won't open.**

9. **Imitate your gym teacher leading exercises.**

10. **Do jumping jacks while singing the *Family Ties* theme song.**

YOU BE THE FORTUNE-TELLER

Hmmm . . . I see that you will live a long life, with a famous Hollywood hunk. He will sweep you off your feet, and carry you away to his huge mansion, where you will never have to clean your room again!

Try these just-for-fun palm-reading techniques. They're a lot of laughs.

Line Up!

To read your subject's palm, hold her left hand, palm up. With your thumb, gently rub the middle of her palm. This will make the lines easier to see.

Take a look at the three most prominent lines. These lines represent the head, the heart, and life. (See diagram on following page.) Each line should be considered in three equal parts, each representing twenty-five years of life. The first segment is youth, the second middle age, and the third old age.

The Lifeline

The most important line begins at the side of the palm between the thumb and first finger and runs down along the base of the thumb. The lifeline shows more than just the length of life.

23

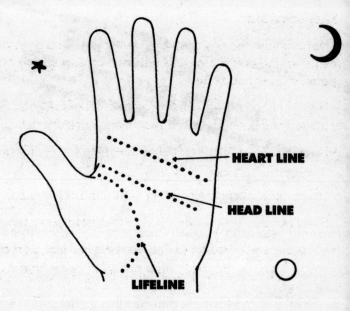

HEART LINE

HEAD LINE

LIFELINE

- Long and well-marked lifeline—good health, average life span.

- Short and strong lifeline—this girl has strong drive, recovers easily from health problems.

- Thin and wavy lifeline—this subject will have many changes in her life.

- Lifeline is long and curved around the base—this girl will still be running around when she is old.

- The lifeline crosses the palm and goes all the way to the other side of the palm—travel will always play a part in this subject's life.

The Head Line

The head line starts at the top of the lifeline and goes across the center of the palm. If there is only one crosswise line on the palm, it is the head line.

• Head line joined with lifeline at the start of the head line—this person is a cautious one who thinks before she acts.

• Head line is separate from lifeline at the start—this girl is adventurous.

• Long, deep, straight head line—the subject is logical.

• Short head line—this girl rarely looks before she leaps.

• Long and upcurved head line—the subject has a great memory.

• Long and downcurved head line—this girl is creative and imaginative.

The Heart Line

• If there are two crosslines on the palm, the top one, parallel to the head line, is the heart line.

• No heart line—the person's mind controls her emotions completely.

• Long heart line—this girl is an idealist who will marry into money.

• Heart line straight and parallel to head line—the person is controlled by her emotions.

• Curved and long heart line—the subject is a romantic.

• Long and deep heart line—this girl is a loyal friend.

SECRET SILLY TALK

If you want to tell secrets and be sure they stay that way, nothing works better than a secret language. Use this secret language whenever you want something to be just between you and your sleepover pals. No one will be able to crack the code.

The secret language isn't hard to understand—once you know the secret. It's a lot like pig latin, but with a special twist that will keep 'em guessing.

Here's how you do it. Divide any word into its syllables. Drop the first consonants of the syllable. Say it and then put the consonants back and add *abo*. Do the same with the next syllables.

Let's try the word *boyfriend*. Oy-babo iend-frabo. Easy!

If the word starts with a vowel, and is only one syllable, just add "abo" to it. For example: *at* is at-abo. If the word has two syllables, deal with each syllable as a separate word. For example: *author* is auth-abo or-abo, *another* is an-abo oth-abo er-abo. *Antler* is ant-abo er-labo.

If a word is just one vowel, add abo to it—*a* is *a-abo* and *I* is I-abo. The letter *y* is pronounced the same as the word *why*.

Let's try some sentences.
The sentence is: You are my best friend.
Ou-yabo are-abo y-mabo est-babo iend-frabo.
How about this one?
The sentence is: Never tell anyone about this secret.
Ev-nabo er-abo ell-tabo an-abo y-abo one-abo a-abo
out-babo is-thabo e-sabo et-crabo.
Got it? Good. Now have fun practicing.

It's getting to be about that time, isn't it? The time when your stomach grumbles, and your tastebuds start salivating for something sweet. A sleepover just wouldn't be a sleepover without some fabulous foods to keep you munchin' and crunchin' the night away. This chapter is filled with recipes that no one can resist—quick munchies, sweet munchies, diet munchies, and sinfully rich munchies! Every single recipe is guaranteed to make everyone's tastebuds tingle! Adjust the amounts of food to feed the number of guests in your party. Okay, everyone get your aprons on. Let's get this party cooking!

Munchies by the Handful

These munchies are as quick to make as they are to eat!

Look What's Popping Popcorn!

You will need:

12 cups freshly popped popcorn

8 tablespoons hot melted margarine or butter

½ cup grated Parmesan cheese

½ teaspoon salt

Put the popcorn in a double brown grocery bag. Pour in the butter or margarine, grated cheese, and salt. Shake the bag really hard. Pour the popcorn into a bowl.

Fun and Funky Fruit Salad

You will need:

A watermelon

A cantaloupe

Apples

Bananas

Orange slices

Seedless grapes

Whipped cream

A knife

A fruit scooper or rounded spoon

Have an adult help you cut the watermelon in half. Use the scooper or the rounded spoon to scoop out the watermelon. Save the shell and set the watermelon balls aside. Scoop out the cantaloupe and set the cantaloupe balls aside, too. Cut the apples, bananas, and oranges into slices. Put all the cut fruit plus the grapes into the watermelon shell and serve. The whipped cream really tops the fruit off!

    (Note: Skip the cream and this snack is perfect for a dieting pal.)

Simply Scrumptious Sleepover Sandwiches!

No well-bread sleepover would be complete without these!

Creamy Cutups!

You will need:

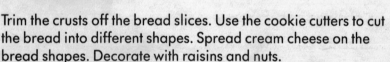

> **8 slices of bread**
>
> **Soft cream cheese**
>
> **Raisins**
>
> **Chopped nuts**
>
> **A knife**
>
> **Cookie cutters**

Trim the crusts off the bread slices. Use the cookie cutters to cut the bread into different shapes. Spread cream cheese on the bread shapes. Decorate with raisins and nuts.

Peanut Butter Pleasers

You will need:

> **Bread**
>
> **Peanut butter**
>
> **Honey**
>
> **A knife**
>
> **A rolling pin**
>
> **Toothpicks**

Cut the crusts off the bread slices. Put each slice on a hard surface. Use the rolling pin to roll the bread out flat. Spread a thin layer of peanut butter on each flattened slice of bread.

Spread some honey over the peanut butter. Roll each piece of bread from the bottom up, making sure the honey and peanut butter are inside. Slice each roll into pieces that are about ¾ of an inch thick. Use the toothpicks to hold each roll together.

Pizzarific Do-It-Yourself Pizzas!

These perky pizzas are perfect every time!

You will need:

Half of a hero roll for each girl

Jars or cans of tomato sauce

Cheddar and/or mozzarella cheese

Sliced pepperoni

Chopped red peppers

Mushrooms (cut in half)

Chopped onion

Cooked meatballs

Oregano

Garlic powder

Everyone gets half a hero roll and a plate. After that it's every girl for herself when it comes to making a dream pizza with the works. Scoop out the soft inside of the roll to make a bread boat. Now start adding just the right amount of sauce, cheese, and toppings.

Preheat oven to 350 degrees. As soon as the custom-made pizzas are complete, place them on a cookie sheet or piece of aluminum foil and pop them in the oven. Bake the pizzas until the cheese melts and the sauce is hot. Then carefully remove them from the oven and serve while hot.

Chocolate Charmers

These chocolate treats will tame even the wildest chocoholic!

Forbidden Fudge

You will need:

1½ cups granulated sugar

½ teaspoon salt

2 tablespoons butter or margarine

½ cup evaporated milk

2 cups semisweet chocolate chips

¾ cup chopped nuts

1½ teaspoons vanilla extract

An 8-inch-square baking pan

A long spoon

A saucepan

Grease the baking pan. Use the spoon to mix the sugar, salt, butter or margarine, and milk in the saucepan. Heat the mixture over medium heat for five minutes. Be sure to stir the mixture all the time. (Don't let it boil.) Take the saucepan off the heat. Add the chocolate chips right away, stirring until they melt into the mixture. Add the nuts and the vanilla. Stir. Pour the mixture into the pan and allow it to cool in the refrigerator for two hours. Cut the fudge into squares.

The Cloud's Sweet Lining!

You will need:

One can of pressurized whipped cream

One box of chocolate wafer cookies

Colored sprinkles

A knife

A narrow dish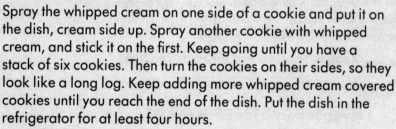

Spray the whipped cream on one side of a cookie and put it on the dish, cream side up. Spray another cookie with whipped cream, and stick it on the first. Keep going until you have a stack of six cookies. Then turn the cookies on their sides, so they look like a long log. Keep adding more whipped cream covered cookies until you reach the end of the dish. Put the dish in the refrigerator for at least four hours.

When you are ready to serve this treat, cover the cookies completely with whipped cream. Add the colored sprinkles. Cut the cookie log on a diagonal to show the cookies and cream stripes. (This serves six.)

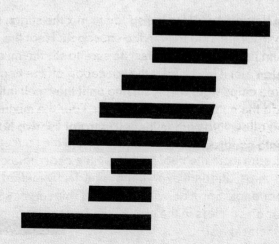

Egg-zactly Egg Cream Chocolate Drink

You will need:

3 tablespoons chocolate syrup

½ cup milk

Club soda or seltzer

A glass

A long spoon

Stir the chocolate syrup and the milk together in a glass. Add the club soda or seltzer very slowly and stir with a long spoon until there is a smooth, fine film on top.

Bananarific!

You will need:

1 large banana for each guest

¾ cup heavy cream

3 ounces chopped semisweet chocolate

8 ounces peanut butter chips

Chopped unsalted peanuts

Plastic wrap

Saucepan

Long spoon

Wrap each banana in plastic wrap. Leave in the freezer for several hours. Heat the cream nearly to a boil in the saucepan. Remove the cream from the heat and stir in the chocolate and peanut butter chips. Stir until everything is perfectly melted. Pour over frozen bananas. Sprinkle with peanuts. (This serves six.)

(Note: For any dieters in the crowd, the frozen bananas are terrific all by themselves!)

The Morning After

Even the best sleepovers must come to an end. But parting will be really sweet sorrow if you start tomorrow off with these chewy, gooey pancakes.

Chip-Chip-Hooray Pancakes!

You will need:

- ¼ cup butter or margarine
- 1½ cups all-purpose flour
- 1 teaspoon baking soda
- ¼ cup granulated sugar
- ½ teaspoon salt
- ¼ cup cocoa
- 2 eggs
- 1 cup milk
- ½ cup milk-chocolate chips

Melt the butter or margarine in a small saucepan over low heat. Set aside to cool. Sift the flour, baking soda, sugar, salt, and cocoa into a large bowl. Break the eggs in another bowl. Beat them slightly with a fork, add the milk, and stir. Add the egg mixture to the flour mixture. Mix well. Slowly stir in the chocolate chips and the melted butter or margarine. Lightly grease a frying pan or griddle and place it on low heat. Once the griddle is hot, spoon the pancake batter onto it. Make each pancake small— about two tablespoons per pancake should be plenty. When the top of a pancake begins to bubble, flip it over. Cook each pancake until both sides are lightly browned. Serve hot, with butter or whipped cream on top. (This serves eight.)

LATE-NIGHT LAUGHS

Ha ha ha ha! Hee hee hee! Are you and your friends starting to laugh a lot more than usual? Relax, you don't have some contagious laughing-hyena disease. Everyone gets silly at a sleepover. To add to the silliness, here are some super stunts and goofy games that are guaranteed to give you the giggles!

Ha, Ha!

This game's been around for as long as girls have been going to sleepovers. It leaves 'em laughing every time.

To play Ha, Ha, everyone has to lie on the floor in a line. Each girl puts her head on the stomach of the girl in front of her.

Now that everyone is settled, the first girl in the line has to say "Ha!" The next girl says "Ha, ha!" The third girl says "Ha, ha, ha!" Keep it up until you reach the end of the line. Then keep the ha, ha's going by starting at the top again. Before you know it, you'll be laughing so hard you'll lose count of the ha's. By that time no one will care—after all, it's the laughter you're after!

Straight Face

If the jokes are great, this game won't leave a straight face in the place.

Everyone picks a partner. One person in each pair will be the joke teller. The other will be the silent partner. It is the joke teller's job to make the silent partner break out laughing. It is the silent partner's job to stay silent and not even break a smile.

The joke teller can tell jokes, make funny faces or funny sounds—everything but tickling or touching the silent partner is allowed.

To make the joke teller's job a little easier, here's a group of side-splitting groaners and gigglers.

How do you keep a skunk from smelling?
Hold its nose!

Why did the umpire throw the chicken out of the game?
He suspected fowl play!

Why did the prisoner eat lots of chocolate?
He was hoping he'd break out!

Why did the crook put the money in the freezer?
He wanted some cold cash!

What kind of car does Michael Jackson drive?
A rock and Rolls-Royce!

Can giraffes have babies?
No, they can only have giraffes.

Is it okay to eat desert sand?
Why eat sand when you can get dirt cheap?!

What did the movie star do to avoid getting wrinkles?
She stopped sleeping in her clothes!

How many sheep does it take to knit a sweater?
None. Sheep can't knit!

What month was King Kong born in?
Ape-ril!

What do you get if you aim your blow dryer down a rabbit hole?
Hot cross bunnies!

Where was the Declaration of Independence signed?
At the bottom!

What do you call it when a vampire kisses you goodnight?
Necking!

What shampoo works best on mountains?
Head and Boulders!

Why can't a leopard hide from hunters?
Wherever it is, a leopard is sure to be spotted!

Handy Laugh Maker

Oh no! What is that silence? Is the laughter starting to die down? No problem. The Handy Laugh Maker will get those giggles going again. This great gag is the goofiest ever!

One person stands up straight with her hands behind her back. Another girl kneels behind the girl that is standing, making sure no one can see her. The girl who is kneeling slips her hands through the standing girl's arms so that the kneeling girl's hands look like they are really the standing girl's hands.

As the standing girl talks, the kneeling girl moves her hands. She can scratch, clap, fix her hair, anything! The important thing is to keep those hands moving. Some fun things to talk about are fixing your hair, brushing your teeth, putting on make-up, or cooking. Those are all things that can be best described with lots of hand motions. No matter what you talk about, the results of this stunt are sure to be hilarious!

Let's Twist Again!

Tongue twisters are always fun. But they're even more fun when you add a new twist and really twist the twisters.

Everybody sits in a circle. The first girl whispers a tongue twister into the second girl's ear. Then the second girl whispers what she heard to the next person, and so on, all the way down the line. The last person in the line has to say the twisted twister out loud.

Try letting everyone have a chance to be first and last in line. To get you started, here are some twicky twisters.

Three tricky tigers timidly tipped ten tall trees.

Sweet suckers soothe suffering skunks.

The black bug bit the big black bear on the big black bear's behind!

Simple Sheila sells seashells by the seashore.

Dull dark dogs don't dig dirt.

Moses supposes his toeses are roses.

Reel to Reel Laughs!

Don't worry, you haven't had the last laugh yet! For some real laughs, just turn out the lights and put on one of these funny video movies. The laughs will last and last.

1. **ABBOTT AND COSTELLO MEET THE INVISIBLE MAN.** In this side splitter, Bud Abbott and Lou Costello play detectives who help out a boxer who's been framed.

2. **THE ABSENT-MINDED PROFESSOR.** Fred MacMurray makes this funny film fly high when he invents flubber—flying rubber.

3. **ADVENTURES IN BABY-SITTING.** Baby-sitting sounds like a nice quiet activity for a Saturday night, right? Wrong! In this hysterical movie a baby-sitter and her charges are in for a nutty night of fun and adventure in Chicago as they run into a gang of car thieves, a frat party, a rhythm and blues nightclub, and a fancy office party. *Adventures in Baby-Sitting* is an adventure in laughter!

4. **BACK TO THE FUTURE.** Michael J. Fox plays an eighties teen who goes back in time and gets stuck in the 1950s. He's got to get his folks together—otherwise, he won't ever be born!

5. **BEDTIME FOR BONZO.** President Ronald Reagan stars in this movie, but you'll go ape for Bonzo, a chimpanzee, whom Ronald Reagan brings into his house as part of a science experiment.

6. **THE BREAKFAST CLUB.** If a film stars Emilio Estevez, Molly Ringwald, Ally Sheedy, and Judd Nelson, what else do you need to know?

7. GHOSTBUSTERS. Bill Murray, Dan Ackroyd, and Harold Ramis are out to catch all the ghosts in New York City. Watch this film and the laughter is sure to catch on!

8. THE MAN WITH TWO BRAINS. What happens when a scientist falls in love with a talking brain inside a jar? You'll wish you had two mouths to laugh with when you watch this Steve Martin giggler.

9. MODERN TIMES. When it comes to funny movies, Charlie Chaplin is the one who really started it all. This silent film is Charlie's best!

10. THE MONEY PIT. Never judge a house by its cover. When Shelley Long and Tom Hanks buy a beautiful house, they have no idea that the stairs will fall, the water will stop flowing, and the living room floor will cave in. You'll laugh out loud at this silly slapstick story.

11. MONKEY BUSINESS. Those zany Marx Brothers, Groucho, Chico, and Harpo, monkey around with the opera in this, their wackiest film. This movie is filled with funny business from beginning to end!

12. MUNSTER, GO HOME. So you like the old TV series starring the gang from 1313 Mockingbird Lane. If you're crazy for the show, you'll go nuts over this movie. Herman, Lily, Grandpa, Eddie, and of course, Marilyn, fly to England to claim a spooky old castle they've inherited. Jolly old England will never be the same.

13. THE MUPPET MOVIE. This is the first and best of the movies featuring Kermit, Miss Piggy, and Jim Henson's other wild characters. This movie tells Kermit's life story. Watch for the bicycle scene—it's amazing!

14. OUTRAGEOUS FORTUNE. Bette Midler and Shelley Long are certainly outrageous in this wild movie. Unfortunately for them, they're both in love with the same guy. Fortunately for us, this sends the wacky duo on a wild adventure that'll leave you laughing for days.

15. POLICE ACADEMY. Not laughing is a real crime when you watch this really arresting movie about a group of crazies who want to be policemen!

16. SIXTEEN CANDLES. Poor Molly Ringwald. Her parents have forgotten her birthday, her grandparents have taken over her room, and the school geek won't leave her alone. *Sixteen Candles* is one sweet comedy!

17. SPACEBALLS. Mel Brooks takes a hilarious look at science fiction movies in his typically zany style. Sit back and enjoy, and "May the Schwartz be with you."

18. TEEN WOLF. As if being a teenager with a really bizarre family wasn't enough, poor Michael J. Fox finds out that he's part werewolf! This funny film is sure to make you roar!

19. THE THREE STOOGES IN ORBIT. Larry, Moe, and Joe wind up flying around the universe in this really spacey flick.

20. YOUNG FRANKENSTEIN. Gene Wilder is the mad scientist in the crazy Mel Brooks take-off of *Frankenstein*.

There are no auditions for a sleepover talent show. You don't have to know how to sing. You don't have to know how to dance. All you need is some good material and a little nerve. Everything you'll ever need to be a sleepover star is right here in this chapter! Okay, everybody, check your make up, and study these scripts. The curtain goes up in five minutes.

The Silent (Movie) Treatment

Silence is golden—especially when it comes to sleepover silent movie skits!

It's easy to turn your living room into an old-fashioned silent movie theater. All you need is a little audience participation. Everyone in the audience should aim their flashlights at the stage. Then the audience members should wave their flashlights up and down really fast. The flickering of the flashlights will make the actors' movements look like an old-fashioned silent movie.

Here are some silent skits that will have the audience screaming for more!

(Note: Since the actors cannot speak, all their lines will be written on cards. For each of these skits, the cast should write the dialogue on large cards before the performance. The Card Holder will hold the cards up, in order, for the audience to see.)

On the Right Track

Scene: The railroad tracks
Cast: Sweet Susan Sorrow
Evil Eric Eerie
Heroic Harold Hornblower
Card Holder

Sweet Susan Sorrow is tied to the railroad tracks! Evil Eric Eerie stands above her!

Eric pretends to speak to her as he curls his mustache. The Card Holder carries a sign saying: "You are done for! The train will run you over and no one will save you!"

Sweet Susan puts her hand to her head in fear. The Card Holder comes back with a sign that reads: "How can you be so evil?"

Eric smiles at her, tweaks his mustache again, and jumps out of the way. The Card Holder's new sign says: "I guess it's my train-ing. And speaking of trains . . ." Eric points to the oncoming train and runs away.

Enter Heroic Harold Hornblower, fixing his always-perfect hair. Card Holder's new sign says: "Sweet Susan, come see my latest dye job."

Sweet Susan puts her hands to her mouth to make a megaphone. The Card Holder's sign says: "I'm a little tied up right now!"

Heroic Harold runs to her rescue, untying her. She hugs him and clutches her heart. The Card Holder's sign says: "My hero!"

Heroic Harold pulls hairspray from under his shirt. The Card Holder's sign says: "And my hair is still perfect, thanks to Sticky Stuff Spray!"

The End

Just Hanging Around

Scene: The window ledge of a tall
building
Cast: Evil Eric Eerie
Sweet Susan Sorrow
Heroic Harold Hornblower
The Card Holder

Sweet Susan Sorrow is hanging from a window ledge. Evil Eric
Eerie is about to pry her fingers loose, and she will fall to her
death.

(Note: You can do this by having Sweet Susan hang on to the
side of a chair.)

Eric twirls his mustache, takes a bite of a chocolate bar, and
smiles an evil grin at Sweet Susan. The Card Holder's card
reads: "I told you not to get your chocolate in my peanut butter!
Now you are done for!"

Sweet Susan looks up at him with fear. The Card Holder's
sign reads: "You'll never get me to fall for you!"

Eric begins to peel her fingers off the ledge when . . .

Enter Heroic Harold Hornblower!

Harold hits Eric, Eric topples, but doesn't fall. Eric hits
Harold. Harold hits Eric. Eric swings at Harold, but misses and
falls to his death.

Harold looks down at Susan. The Card Holder's sign reads:
"What are you doing there?"

Susan looks up at him pleadingly. The Card Holder's sign
says: "Oh, just hanging around."

Harold picks Susan up.

Susan clutches her heart. The Card Holder's sign reads: "My
hero!"

Heroic Harold Hornblower looks at his shirt and looks
angry. The Card Holder's sign reads: "That villain! He got his
chocolate on my shirt!"

Susan smiles at him. The Card Holder's sign reads: "I can

get it out with Charge—the stain remover of heroes!"

Heroic Harold hugs Susan. The Card Holder's sign reads: "You saved my shirt. You are my heroine!"

Super Sleepover Skits

These silly skits may give acting a bad name, but they are sure to give your audience a good case of the giggles! In fact, some of these skits are filled with so many groaners that your audience may ask you to get your act together and take it on the road— say, to another state!

Food for Thought

Scene: A restaurant
Cast: The waitress
Customer 1
Customer 2
The thief

Two customers are sitting at the table. The waitress, who has just served the meal, is standing over them.

Customer 1: Waitress, what is this fly doing in my soup?

Waitress (looking in the soup): I believe it's the backstroke, madam.

Customer 1: And what is this leatherlike stuff on my plate?

Waitress: I believe it is filet of sole, madam.

Customer 1: Well, can't I have something a little softer from the top part of the shoe?

Customer 2: May I change this tomato for another vegetable?

Waitress (throwing the tomato in the air and letting it fall on the table): Here.

Customer 2: I asked for another vegetable. What's this?

Waitress: I threw the tomato in the air and it came down . . . squash!

Thief (running over to the customer): All right! Hands up!

Waitress (with her hands in the air): You thief! What do you think you're doing?

Thief: Stealing this scene, of course!

The End

Schoolroom Silliness

Scene: A classroom
Cast: Jenny
      Wendy
      Cathy
      Teacher

The girls are seated in a row. The teacher is at the front of the room.

Teacher: Jenny, name the four seasons.

Jenny: Salt, sugar, pepper, and spice!

Teacher: Wendy, if you have nine potatoes and must divide them equally between six people, how would you do it?

Wendy: I'd mash 'em!

Teacher: Cathy, name five things that contain milk.

Cathy: Ice cream, butter, cheese, and two cows!

Teacher: Jenny, can you spell mouse?

Jenny: M-O-U-S.

Teacher: What's at the end of it?

Jenny: A tail!

The bell rings, the girls get up to leave.

Teacher: Well, class, how do you like school?

Girls (in unison): CLOSED!

The End

Look Who's Talking

Scene: The stage
Cast: Ventriloquist
Wooden Wilma (a ventriloquist's dummy)
Props: A glass of water

Wooden Wilma is sitting on the ventriloquist's knee.

Ventriloquist (to audience): Hello, I am a ventriloquist, and this is my dummy, Wooden Wilma. So, Wooden Wilma, I hear you visited your cousin's farm. Did you have a good time?

Wooden Wilma: Sure. I was real busy. After my visit that farm will never be the same.

Ventriloquist: How so?

Wooden Wilma: Well, I made the slowest horse on the farm fast.

Ventriloquist: That's amazing! How did you do that?

Wooden Wilma: I took away his food!

Ventriloquist: What else did you do on the farm?

Wooden Wilma: I took care of the chickens. You haven't done anything until you've chased chickens with six feet!

Ventriloquist: Chickens with six feet! Since when do chickens have six feet?

Wooden Wilma: When there are three of them!

Ventriloquist: How did you get to be so sarcastic? (Ventriloquist starts to drink water as Wooden Wilma talks)

Wooden Wilma: I've had a few hard knocks. (Watching as ventriloquist drinks water) Hey! I am amazed! You finally learned how to do that!

Ventriloquist: What—drink while you talk?

Wooden Wilma: No, drink without dribbling water all over your shirt!

Ventriloquist (sarcastically): Very funny! Now I have a joke for you. Knock knock.

Wooden Wilma: I love knock-knock jokes! They remind me of my Uncle Woody.

Ventriloquist: Oh, did he tell knock-knock jokes?

Wooden Wilma: No, he was a door!

Ventriloquist: Knock knock!

Wooden Wilma: Who's there?

Ventriloquist: Wilby.

Wooden Wilma: Wilby who?

Ventriloquist: We'll be seeing ya! (Both wave good-bye)

Haunted Ha-ha's!

Scene: A haunted house
Cast: Witch 1
       Witch 2
       Witch 3

The witches are mixing a brew.

Witch 1: Cooking for a party is such fun. Let's see, this recipe calls for a little eye of newt, some worm's guts, some frog's legs . . .

Witch 2: No, hold the frog's legs. I'm on a diet!

Witch 3: Let me make the brew. I was number one in witch school, you know.

Witch 1: We know, you were the best *spell*-er!

Witch 2: Hurry with that brew, the guests will be here soon. I'll start the omelets. By the way, how do ghosts like their eggs?

Witch 3: Terri-fried.

Witch 1: We'd better get the music ready. I do hope Sam the Skeleton will dance this year. He never does.

Witch 2: What do you expect? He never has any-*body* to dance with!
(All three witches cackle)

Witch 3: I do hope the party is a success! I was so bored at the ghosts' last bash.

Witch 2: I remember. We all sat around and told people stories!

The End

Lip-Synch or Swim

So you want to be a rock 'n' roll star! Well, we can't guarantee you a gig singing at a huge arena, but we can guarantee that this fun performance game will have you and your friends rocking 'n' rolling with laughter.

Everybody splits up into groups. Then each group looks through the hostess's record and tape collection and chooses a song to perform.

Put on the record and let the group mouth the words to the song along with the real singers. Some of the members of the group can dance, while others play the invisible guitar, invisible horn, or invisible drums. Let the audience vote on the group that gives the best show.

Here are some hints for a performance that is sure to rock them right out of their seats.

1. Round hair brushes make great microphones. Real rock 'n' roll stars use their mikes as props—you should, too!

2. Two pencils make great drumsticks for air drumming. Remember, don't hit anything with them—the noise won't match what's on the record. Try to flip your sticks in the air, just like a real drummer.

3. Lots of rock stars wear wild clothes on stage. If you don't have long scarves and headbands around, use toilet paper or streamers—after all, this is make-believe!

4. Try to imitate your favorite stars as closely as possible. Here are some stars that are easy to imitate.
   • Billy Joel likes to stand up and bang on his piano.
   • Whitney Houston swings her arms in time to the music as if

she's really ready to Dance With Somebody. Don't forget to smile!

- Michael Jackson rarely wears his glove in concert anymore, but he still does that famous moon walk!
- When Clarence Clemmons plays his sax at a Bruce Springsteen concert, he's sure to throw his head back before he blows!
- Jon Bon Jovi shakes that wild mane of hair all over whenever he lets rip with a song.

You've seen many other favorite stars sing in videos. Just pick your favorite and do whatever he or she does.

FRIGHT NIGHT

It's late at night. Just the right time for ghosts and goblins to come out and haunt your sleepover! But they are very welcome guests. Let's face it, no sleepover is ever complete without some scary stuff going on.

The Tale of the Black Cat

Here's a spooky story. Read it aloud if you dare! But be warned—this tale is guaranteed to scare you out of your wits! Heh-heh-heh-heh-heh!

This is a true story that happened many years ago, in a small town not far from here. The town was surrounded on all sides by dark, thick woods. Not even the bravest men would venture into that forest at night, because even during a full moon, no light could reach through the trees. The people of the town were sure that the woods were haunted!

The only person who wasn't afraid of the treacherous forest was the Widow Clancy. She lived in a small cottage deep in the forest behind many tall, thick evergreens. Her husband had died thirty years before, but she stayed, all alone, in the cottage he had built for her. Few people saw the widow much anymore; she only came into town for the few groceries she needed.

When she did come into town, the people talked. The widow always dressed in black and let her long black hair fall in a tangle around her shoulders. She never spoke to anyone. And the odd groceries she bought! She would go to the bait store for small fish, frogs, and worms. She would go to the pet shop and buy a great deal of cat food.

The cat food was especially strange, since in all the years the widow had lived in the town, no one had ever seen her with a cat. Not even the veterinarian—and he knew all the animals in the tiny community.

But the thing that disturbed the townspeople the most was the way the Widow Clancy would take a shortcut through the cemetery on her way back to her cottage. No one else would dare cut through the cemetery. But the widow seemed to enjoy it. She was seen smiling and laughing with that cackling laugh she always had, as she made her way past the tombstones.

A group of girls in the town were especially fascinated by the Widow Clancy. One afternoon they all gathered in the park to discuss the old lady.

"She's a witch!" Amy Anderson said to the others.

"She puts spells on people," said Julie Saunders.

"We have to get rid of her!" cried Lizzie Saunders, Julie's younger sister.

But Katharine Sacks was still. She really didn't want to know about the Widow Clancy. She was too scared.

"I say we find out what this widow is really about. I say we go to spy on her tonight!" Amy declared.

The girls were all in agreement. All, that is, except Katharine Sacks. But she let her friends coax her into going along. That was her first big mistake!

That night the sky was very dark and cloudy. Katharine looked out her bedroom window and prayed that the others would decide not to go into the woods on such an ominous night. But as soon as the clock by her bedside struck eleven, she heard three stones hit her window. The signal! Carefully carrying her flashlight, Katharine slipped out the window and jumped to the garden below.

Shutting her ears to the cry of the wind, Katharine followed Amy, Julie, and Lizzie into the black dungeon which was the forest.

The forest was frightening at night. By the light of the flashlights, the tree branches looked like bony skeleton arms, grabbing for the girls and tearing through their hair. And soft and insistent, a voice in the wind cried, "Turn back . . . turn back . . ."

Finally the girls reached the house. It was almost completely dark, but a tiny light flickered in the window. They crept closer and peeked in. They saw the Widow Clancy cooking a large stew over a flame in the fireplace. She was stirring the liquid in the pot and talking to herself.

"Why, she's nothing but a crazy old lady," Julie said to Lizzie. "Look at her, talking to herself."

Just then, Katharine dropped her flashlight in the leaves. The noise startled the Widow Clancy, and she turned to see the four girls in the window. Suddenly the light in the fireplace went out and a large black cat jumped out the window and clawed at Katharine. Screaming, the girls ran for their lives out of the forest and back to their homes!

That night, the girls crept back into their beds as if nothing had happened. Nothing seemed odd or out of sorts. But the next morning Mrs. Anderson ran screaming into the town square.

"My Amy is gone!" she cried.

Julie, Lizzie, and Katharine ran to Amy's room. Her bed looked as though she'd slept in it, but their friend had disappeared!

The police had no idea what could have happened to Amy. Their only clues were a black hair, left near Amy's satin pillow, and the state of the pillow itself. The pillow had been ripped apart, as though a cat had gotten into the room and used its claws to rip the satin.

The next night, Katharine, Lizzie, and Julie went to sleep, the same as they did every night. Katharine heard the wind rustling through the trees outside her bedroom, and was reminded of the awful trip through the woods. She didn't sleep a wink all night.

The very next morning Lizzie and Julie were discovered missing. Just as in Amy's disappearance, the police had only two clues to the crime—a single black hair on each of the girls pillows and two pillows torn apart by a cat's violent claws.

Katharine was afraid to shut her eyes that night. She knew she was next. Still, sleep began to overtake her until she heard a quiet rustling on her windowsill. Afraid to open her eyes, Katharine shivered in her bed as she heard the window creak open and small footsteps land cautiously on her bed.

Suddenly a large black cat leaped onto Katharine's stomach. Katharine could hardly breathe. She gasped for breath. Expertly, the cat placed a delicate paw over Katharine's mouth and wrapped its long tail around Katharine's body, squeezing her arms to her sides so that the girl could not move. This was no ordinary cat! This cat had more strength than ten men! Katharine felt woozy, the air was being forced out of her lungs; she could not move. Desperate, Katharine bit at the cat's paw. The cat screeched and leaped off the bed! Black smoke billowed throughout the room. When the smoke cleared, Katharine stared in shock! There stood the Widow Clancy! Beside her were Amy, Julie, and Lizzie. The three girls rubbed their eyes in disbelief!

"Wh-what happened?" Lizzie cried. The girls all looked at the widow.

"What kind of awful creature are you?" Amy cried to the old woman.

But the widow grabbed her bleeding hand and jumped from the bedroom window. The only answer she left for the girls to ponder was a single long black hair on the windowsill!

The next day, when the Widow Clancy came to town for her shopping, she had a bandage around her right hand. And until the end of her days she would never explain the wound to anyone!

Things went back to normal, except that every night, as soon as she shut her eyes, each girl would hear a soft purring, growing louder and louder, until the morning sun rose. Nothing would block it out. Over and over, "Meow ... Meow ... Meow ... MEOW!"

A Haunting Effect!

You'll see ghosts in the shadows when you try these scary shadow pictures. They'll drive you up a wall! Everybody get your flashlights. It's time to turn this ordinary house in an ordinary neighborhood into a haunted mansion!

To make scary shadow pictures, start by turning out all the lights. Shine a flashlight on a blank wall. The light should be a few feet behind your hands. Move close enough to the wall to make sure your shadow pictures can be seen clearly, but don't get so close that no one else can see them.

Use your hands to imitate the drawings below. But be careful—some shadow goblins may want to stay at the sleepover, long after all the lights are out!

THE BAT

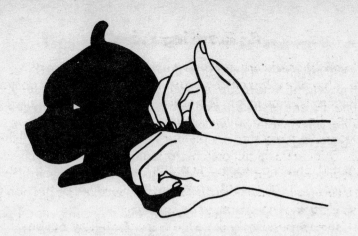

THE GOBLIN

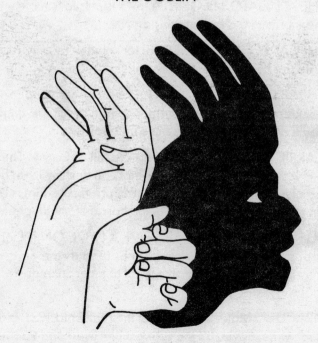

THE GHOST OF THE BEHEADED INDIAN CHIEF

Horrors! Are We Out of Popcorn?

If you still haven't had enough of things that go bump in the night, now is the time to turn on your VCR and pop in a creepy cassette. Try one of the ones on this list. They're all guaranteed to scare the wits out of even the most die-hard horror-movie fan! They're a scream!

1. ALIEN. This is a space-age scarer! A spacecraft is carrying a deadly creature that grows inside the human body.

2. ALIENS. This is the sequel to *Alien*, and it's even better. This time Sigourney Weaver goes back to battle the creatures that killed her crew. Hold on to your space seats!

3. THE ALLIGATOR PEOPLE. A town is in true trouble when a man turns into a human alligator!

4. THE BAT PEOPLE. When a doctor is bitten by a flying creature he goes absolutely batty!

5. THE BIRDS. Birds go beserk and start ganging up (or is that flocking up) on humans. Feathers fly in this spine-tingler. You'll never look at birds the same way again.

6. CARRIE. Everyone in school makes fun of Carrie. They don't know she has special powers that can destroy them all. She gets her evil revenge at the school prom. This film is based on a thriller by the master of the horror story, Stephen King!

7. THE CREATURE FROM THE BLACK LAGOON. When a group of scientists go on a journey to study the Amazon, they have no idea they are about to meet an underwater monster!

8. DRACULA. Make sure you get the really old 1931, black-and-white movie. It's the scariest film ever made about the cunning count who is really a vampire searching for fresh blood.

9. DR. JEKYLL AND MR. HYDE. There are lots of versions of this chiller, and they are all terrific—take whatever's in the video store. Dr. Jekyll is a nice gentle man. His evil side, Mr. Hyde, is capable of all sorts of evil, including murder!

10. FRANKENSTEIN. Just like *Dracula*, the oldies are the real goodies. If you want to see the ultimate monster movie, you'll have to rent the 1931 version of *Frankenstein*, starring Boris Karloff. Don't see this one alone!

11. GODZILLA—KING OF THE MONSTERS. A fire-breathing dragon is taking over the world!

12. HOUSE OF WAX. Vincent Price, that star of scary stories, plays the owner of a wax museum that uses human victims as sculptures.

13. THE INCREDIBLE SHRINKING MAN. A scientist's secret formula keeps shrinking him, smaller, and smaller, and smaller.

14. INVASION OF THE BODY SNATCHERS. There are two movie versions of this scary story. The original is from 1956 and is in black and white. The remake was released in 1978 and is in color. It doesn't matter which one you see; the story of alien beings growing in pods and taking over the minds and bodies of a town of people will keep you on the edge of your seat!

15. KING KONG. This is another film that has been made and remade. In this case, the original is the best. Be sure to rent the 1933 Fay Wray version. You'll shiver in your seat when King Kong grabs the beautiful girl and kidnaps her!

16. THE MONSTER THAT CHALLENGED THE WORLD. A huge water creature wants to take over the earth!

17. **THE MUMMY.** Boris Karloff, the king of creepy creature features, stars as an ancient mummy who is on the loose and seeking a mate! This film will wrap you with chills and thrills!

18. **TEENAGE ZOMBIES.** When a group of teenagers sail to a jungle island, they are greeted by the natives, who turn them into zombies!

19. **THEM!** A nuclear explosion helps giant ants to breed and take over the southwest United States!

20. **THE THING THAT COULDN'T DIE.** A head comes back after a hundred years seeking its body. Use your head—watch this thriller.

SUPER SLEEPOVER PLANNING PAGES

Here's a quick checklist to help you get everything ready for your Super Sleepover.

Pre-party Planning

1. Invitations (Be sure to tell each guest to bring one outfit she really hates and one accessory she really loves. They'll need them for the Fashion Parade on page 17).

Bought _____

Sent

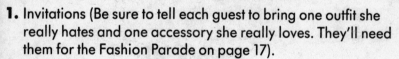

_____

_____

_____

_____

_____

_____

_____

_____

2. RSVPs

_____

_____

_____

_____

_____

_____

_____

Game Stuff

1. Paper

2. Pencils

3. Chairs

4. Board games

_____

_____

_____

_____

Makeover Essentials

1. Shampoo
2. Conditioner
3. Herbs
4. Styling gel
5. Hairspray
6. Coated rubber bands
7. Bobby pins
8. Cleansing soap
9. Cucumber
10. Talcum powder
11. Eye shadows
12. Blush
13. Glitter
14. Emery boards
15. Bowls
16. Extras:

_____

_____

_____

_____

Food Supplies

Check out the recipes on pages 28–35 and put your shopping list here.

1. Munchies

Look What's Popping Popcorn!

Ingredients

_____

_____

_____

_____

Fun and Funky Fruit Salad

Ingredients

_____

_____

_____

_____

2. Scrumptious Sandwiches

Creamy Cutups!

Ingredients

_____

_____

_____

_____

Peanut Butter Pleasers

Ingredients

_____

_____

_____

_____

3. Do-It-Yourself Pizzas

Ingredients

_____

_____

_____

_____

_____

_____

4. Chocolate Charmers

Forbidden Fudge

Ingredients

_____

_____

_____

_____

_____

_____

The Cloud's Sweet Lining!

Ingredients

_____

_____

_____

_____

_____

_____

Egg-zactly Egg Cream Chocolate Drink

Ingredients

_____

_____

_____

_____

_____

_____

Bananarific!

Ingredients

_____

_____

_____

_____

_____

_____

5. Breakfast

Juice

Milk

Hot Chocolate

Chips-Chip-Hooray Pancakes

Ingredients

_____

_____

_____

_____

_____

_____

_____

Videos

1. Funny (See pages 40–42.)

_____

_____

_____

_____

_____

_____

_____

_____

2. Scary (See pages 60–62.)

_____

_____

_____

_____

_____

_____

_____

_____

Other Notes:

_____

_____

_____

_____

_____

_____

_____

_____

_____

_____

_____

_____

_____

_____

_____

_____

_____

_____

_____